ADVANCE: THE DEVOTIONAL

40 DAYS TO UNLEASHING THE IMPOSSIBLE IN YOUR LIFE

CHAD GONZALES

Scripture quotations taken from the New King James Version. (NKJV) Copyright © 1982 by Thomas Nelson, Inc. Used by permission. All rights reserved.

Scripture quotations taken from the Amplified® Bible, (AMPC) Copyright © 1954, 1958, 1962, 1964, 1965, 1987 by The Lockman Foundation. Used by permission." (www.Lockman.org) Scripture quotations taken from the Amplified® Bible (AMP), Copyright © 2015 by The Lockman Foundation. Used by permission. www.lockman.org

Scripture quotations marked (GNT) are from the Good News Translation in Today's English Version- Second Edition Copyright © 1992 by American Bible Society. Used by Permission.

Scripture quotations are taken from the Holy Bible, New Living Translation, copyright ©1996, 2004, 2015 by Tyndale House Foundation. Used by permission of Tyndale House Publishers, Carol Stream, Illinois 60188. All rights reserved.

Scripture taken from THE MESSAGE. Copyright © 1993, 1994, 1995, 1996, 2000,

2001, 2002. Used by permission of NavPress Publishing Group."

ISBN: 978-1-7354232-9-6

Advance The Devotional: A 40-day Guide to Unleashing the Impossible in Your Life Copyright © 2024 by Chad Gonzales www.ChadGonzales.com

Cover design by Lisa Zukoski

All rights reserved.

Copyright © 2024 by Chad Gonzales

All rights reserved.

No part of this book may be reproduced in any form or by any electronic or mechanical means, including information storage and retrieval systems, without written permission from the author, except for the use of brief quotations in a book review.

CONTENTS

Day 1   1
NO IDENTITY, NO ADVANCEMENT

Day 2   5
FILL AND SUBDUE

Day 3   7
THE QUESTION OF YOUR IDENTITY

Day 4   11
RUN TOWARDS THE GIANT

Day 5   13
ERADICATE FEAR

Day 6   15
WALKING THROUGH HELL

Day 7   19
JESUS WAS EXPECTING GREATER

Day 8   21
KNOWING HIS VOICE

Day 9   23
WHAT ARE YOU DESIRING

Day 10   27
THE POWER OF YOUR IMAGINATION

Day 11   31
INSIDER SECRETS

Day 12   35
GROW BEYOND YOUR SENSES

Day 13   37
CONTROL YOUR TEMPER

Day 14   39
GUARD YOUR DREAM

Day 15   43
THEY ARE CHEERING FOR YOU

Day 16   47
NO MORE EXCUSES

Day 17   49
GO FOR GREATER

Day 18   51
GET OUT OF ELEMENTARY SCHOOL

Day 19 *EMBRACE WISDOM*	53
Day 20 *WORK FOR THE LORD*	55
Day 21 *EVERYTHING IS POSSIBLE*	57
Day 22 *WHATEVER YOU SAY*	61
Day 23 *GO TO THE PLACE I WILL SHOW YOU*	65
Day 24 *PUT YOUR FOCUS ON OTHERS*	69
Day 25 *THE CRITICISM OF CRITICS*	71
Day 26 *THE PRAISES OF MEN*	73
Day 27 *BE THANKFUL*	75
Day 28 *FINISH THE WORK*	77
Day 29 *USE YOUR IMAGINATION FOR GOOD*	79
Day 30 *LOVE YOUR ENEMIES*	83
Day 31 *KEEP THE MAIN THING THE MAIN THING*	87
Day 32 *CONSCIOUS OF HIS PRESENCE*	91
Day 33 *STOP CARING*	95
Day 34 *BUILT DIFFERENT*	99
Day 35 *THE HEART OF A GIVER*	101
Day 36 *UNTOUCHABLE*	105
Day 37 *CONFORMED*	107
Day 38 *SURROUND YOURSELF WITH BIG THINKERS*	109

Day 39	111
BE STILL	
Day 40	115
FORGET THE PAST	
About the Author	119
Also by Chad Gonzales	121
The Supernatural Life Podcast	123
The Healing Academy	125
More from CGM	127

DAY 1
NO IDENTITY, NO ADVANCEMENT

Genesis 1:26-27 NKJV
Then God said, "Let Us make man in Our image, according to Our likeness; let them have dominion over the fish of the sea, over the birds of the air, and over the cattle, over all the earth and over every creeping thing that creeps on the earth." So God created man in His own image; in the image of God He created him; male and female He created them.

If you are going to advance in the things of God, you must know who you are. Identity is crucial to advancing; without knowing your identity, you'll never truly know your gifting or your calling. Identity is so important, we find it in the very first chapter of the Bible.

When we read the story of creation in Genesis 1, we see God create the heavens and the earth. God creates the oceans and beaches, the sun, moon and stars, the animals, plants and mountains. Then on day 6, God created mankind. When God created mankind, He didn't make them like the animals. Contrary to the teachings of evolution, man didn't come from a frog or monkey. In Genesis 1:26, God makes man to be like Him!

Notice God says, "Let us make man in our image, according to our likeness." God made us to be like Him. Now don't misunderstand me: we are certainly not all knowing and not omnipresent. We cannot take His place and we are entirely dependent on Him; however, God put us in His class. We must understand this.

In Genesis 1, we see that God created everything to produce after its own kind. An oak tree produces more oak trees, not pine trees. An elephant produces more elephants, not more horses. Within the seed of every animal or plant is the genetic code to produce after its own kind. Did you notice that after God instituted this with the animals and plants, then He began to talk about us? God made us to be like Him.

We even see Jesus talk about this in John 10. The Pharisees were extremely upset with Jesus because He said God was His Father. Jesus' response was simple: He referred them to Psalm 82:6 which says, "You are gods, And all of you are children of the Most High."

Isn't it interesting that in the very first chapter of the Bible, God tells us we are like Him. Then you find King David telling us we are like God. Then Jesus tells us we are like God. Then you even find it towards the end of the Bible in 1 John 4:4 where it says, "You are born of God, little children."

If God is your Father, you have to be like Him and this is what happens when you receive Jesus as your savior and, are born again. You are born of God, made in His image, according to His likeness.

As you begin to understand your true identity, then we begin to understand our possessions and our purpose. You begin to understand your grace and your calling. You begin to understand your purpose in life and can begin to run after it with fervor and intensity. But, friend, this is why there has been such a lull in the Church.

We have separated our identity from our Father God. We call Him Father, but do not identify as His offspring. We stand in our churches and sing of Him being Father and Abba, some even affectionately call Him Papa, and yet when it comes to our lives, it's a stretch to even see Him as a distant relative.

Without knowing your position in this life as a child of God, made in His image, according to His likeness, you'll never understand your possessions and purpose and therefore, will never advance. God revealed their identity first and then gave them a possession and purpose. God made them like Him, blessed them and then commissioned them to advance.

Advancing is not optional — and neither is knowing your identity. If there is no identity, there is no advancement.

DAY 2
FILL AND SUBDUE

Genesis 1:28-NKJV
Then God blessed them, and God said to them, "Be fruitful and multiply; fill the earth and subdue it."

It never was God's plan for Adam and Eve to sit in the garden of Eden, eat the fruit of the trees, hang out with the animals and merely enjoy a vacation in paradise. The rest of the world did not look like the garden and it was their responsibility to go into the world and make it look like the garden. The garden of Eden was an example of Heaven on earth; you could say it was the prototype that Adam and Eve were to use in going throughout the rest of the world.

God gave them a command in Genesis 1:28. For me, this is the original great commission; this was a command by the 5 star general to his soldiers. First God said, "Be fruitful and multiply." The world began with a male and female and God gave them the responsibility of procreating and producing more people.

Secondly, God said, "Fill the earth and subdue it." The word *subdue* in the Hebrew literally means "to bring under your subjection, to make it your slave." What were they to subdue? The earth. They were to tell the animals, the ground, the trees, the mountains — they were to tell them what to do. Now, just hearing that sounds a little strange, doesn't it? But is it considered strange for a woman to give birth to a baby? No. Notice however that in the same command to, "Be fruitful and multiply…", God said, "…fill the earth and subdue it."

Friend, the same grace to have a baby is the same grace to fill the earth with Heaven and make it your slave. We have attributed one to humanity and one to God, but God attributed both to humanity.

Look at the miracles of the Old Testament. You will notice that most of the miracles by Moses, Joshua, Elijah and Elisha are those of subduing the earth — not healing. They divided waters, multiplied food, called fire out of Heaven, and a host of other outrageous miracles. We even see Jesus do the same: turn water into wine, calm storms, walk on water, multiply food and was even tempted to turn rocks into bread.

We have sold ourselves short in our salvation and privilege of being children of God. In the very beginning of time, at the onset of creating mankind, it was God's intention for us to advance — to always be advancing, always increasing and always multiplying. The same ease at which we have babies is the same ease we are to fill the earth with Heaven and subdue it. It is a command of God and yet with every command, there is also the empowerment to fulfill it.

DAY 3
THE QUESTION OF YOUR IDENTITY

Genesis 3:1-6 NKJV
Now the serpent was more cunning than any beast of the field which the Lord God had made. And he said to the woman, "Has God indeed said, 'You shall not eat of every tree of the garden'?" And the woman said to the serpent, "We may eat the fruit of the trees of the garden; but of the fruit of the tree which is in the midst of the garden, God has said, 'You shall not eat it, nor shall you touch it, lest you die.'" Then the serpent said to the woman, "You will not surely die. For God knows that in the day you eat of it your eyes will be opened, and you will be like God, knowing good and evil." So when the woman saw that the tree was good for food, that it was pleasant to the eyes, and a tree desirable to make one wise, she took of its fruit and ate. She also gave to her husband with her, and he ate.

When God gives you a command, it's guaranteed that satan will come your way and try to stop you. But how does he stop you?

It starts with a thought. As a believer, satan has no power over you and such was the case with Eve in the garden of Eden. In Genesis 2:15, God commanded Adam to guard the garden. Adam was the master and satan was the slave and could not do anything that Adam would not allow.

Remember, Adam and Eve had a command to not only have babies and produce more people, but also to fill the earth with Heaven and subdue it. Satan couldn't stop them from doing that either, so he had to tempt them; the goal was that Adam and Eve would stop themselves. The nature of the temptation? It was identity. Satan's temptation was simple. Satan said, "If you will eat of the tree, you will be like God." It was the great deception because in reality, Eve was already made to be like God.

In Genesis 1:26, God said, "Let's make man in our image, according to our likeness." Eve was already made to be like God, but she didn't realize it. So what did she do? She was deceived by satan, and both she and Adam ate of the tree and they both died spiritually. As a result, they no longer were in a position to advance the things of God.

Not only did they die spiritually, we see no repentance on the part of Adam. Instead of accepting blame, Adam blamed his wife, who in turn blamed the serpent. Then, it went from bad to worse! It seems that once they stopped advancing, they started going backwards. After time, they had two boys and at some point, the oldest son killed his brother.

When you stop advancing, you start dying! But you'll never advance in your calling until you first understand your identity. If you know who you are, satan will never be able to make you stumble, but every trick he brings will have identity at its root. Satan's first temptation of man was on identity. Satan's first temptation of Jesus was about his identity and satan's temptations against you will be about your identity.

Know who you are in Christ and you'll never stumble while you are advancing.

DAY 4
RUN TOWARDS THE GIANT

> *1 Samuel 17:46-48 NLT*
> *Today the Lord will conquer you, and I will kill you and cut off your head. And then I will give the dead bodies of your men to the birds and wild animals, and the whole world will know that there is a God in Israel! And everyone assembled here will know that the Lord rescues his people, but not with sword and spear. This is the Lord's battle, and he will give you to us!" As Goliath moved closer to attack, David quickly ran out to meet him.*

I don't care who you are, how anointed you are, or how educated you are, we are all going to face giants in our lives.

Circa 1020 BC, there was a young man named David who was faced with a colossal task of fighting a giant named Goliath.

Goliath was the giant warrior of the Philistines. He was so big and scary, the Israelite army was terrified of him and wasn't willing to advance toward the army. Every day, Goliath came out and taunted the Israelite army, which included David's brothers. I love the story of David and Goliath because I love a good underdog story. David was probably a teenager and had been sent by his father to bring some food to his brothers. While David is in the camp, he hears Goliath's taunts toward the Israelite army. Upon hearing the vile things Goliath says, it angers David. David grabs his sling and walks onto the battlefield. David declares that not only would he kill Goliath, but he will also kill the rest of the Philistine army!

My favorite part of the story is verse 48 that says, "As Goliath moved closer to attack, David quickly ran out to meet him." David didn't sheepishly walk out to the giant; he ran toward him.

There are two keys to advancing that we see from this story.

Number one: what you say is important.

David declared the end from the beginning. Your words can put you over or they can put you under. There is power in your words, and they will ultimately shape your beliefs.

Number two: no giant is too big to kill.

Friend, there is nothing impossible with God. No giant, no storm, no mountain is bigger than our God. If a giant is in front of you, it is because God has empowered you to take it down.

We must never retreat in the face of giants. It's not about the size of the dog in the fight, but about the size of the fight in the dog. When a giant shows up in your life, it is another opportunity to prove that the Word of God is true. It is another opportunity to prove to the world what David proved to the Philistines when he said, "And everyone assembled here will know that the Lord rescues His people, but not with sword and spear. This is the Lord's battle, and he will give you to us!"

We advance not only for God, but so the world will know there is a God!

DAY 5
ERADICATE FEAR

Numbers 13:32-33 NLT
So they spread this bad report about the land among the Israelites: "The land we traveled through and explored will devour anyone who goes to live there. All the people we saw were huge. We even saw giants there, the descendants of Anak. Next to them we felt like grasshoppers, and that's what they thought, too!"

In Numbers 13, we find the Israelites at the edge of the Promised land of Canaan. This was a land that God had not only promised to the Israelites, but God had also told them He had already given it to them— they just needed to go take it. God had already set this thing up!

Not only had God already set up their victory, He also gave them proof of the goodness of the land. Moses had sent twelve men to spy out the land and when they returned, they came back with reports of how great the land was — but they also came back with reports of how greatly fortified the cities were and how big the giants were. What was the result? Instead of recalling the miracles God had performed in the wilderness, ten of the spies focused on the giants. They allowed their faith in God to be swallowed up by fear.

Do you know what fear will do? First of all, fear will make you stupid! You will think stupid, talk stupid and act stupid. The same spies, despite having witnessed God's numerous miracles in Egypt and the parting of the Red Sea, doubted their ability to defeat the giants.

Friend, it doesn't take but just a second of getting your eyes off of God and on to the problem before the problem becomes bigger than your God. As long as God is bigger, you will advance towards what God has promised you, but as soon as you focus on the problem, you will stop advancing and start retreating.

Do you know what happened as a result of the ten evil spies? Their fear of ten men contaminated the camp. Over one million people believed the ten men's report, leading to forty years of wandering in the wilderness. This journey lasted until all the doubters had passed away. At the end of the forty years, God took the children who had grown up, and they went into the promised land and took what God had promised their parents and grandparents.

Never, never, never allow fear to gain a stronghold in your life. Fear will cause you to magnify your problems. Fear will cause you to retreat. Fear will cause you to die.

Fear will paralyze you and stop you in your tracks if you allow it. Fear is the enemy's tool, crafted to halt your advancement. I don't care what you are facing - whether it is financial, physical or relational - don't you quit. Don't you give into fear. Know that the promise of God is greater than the problem and advance towards your promise.

DAY 6
WALKING THROUGH HELL

Psalm 23:4 NLT
Even when I walk through the darkest valley, I will not be afraid, for you are close beside me.

It's guaranteed that when you are advancing, all of hell is going to come against you to endeavor to stop you. Now remember: satan can't stop you, but he will bring storms, persecution and temptations to get you to stop advancing and start retreating.

In Psalm 23, King David writes that even in the darkest moments, he was unafraid. Not only was he not afraid, he kept walking through.

I have been through some serious trials in my life but never have I been through anything as bad as when my first wife Lacy unexpectedly passed away at the young age of forty years old. My son Jake and I were in Fort Worth, Texas, where I was preaching at a church. I'll never forget flying back to Tampa, Florida and getting the call from our county sheriff that Lacy had passed away. Here I was at forty-five years old, with my fourteen-year-old son by my side when, suddenly, my wife of twenty years was now in Heaven.

Talk about walking through hell. We had just experienced arguably our best year of marriage. We were absolutely loving our first year of living in Florida. The reality of Jake getting older had begun to spark excitement and talk of the next phase of life: empty nesters and grandchildren. All of our goals and dreams — in a moment were shattered. I now was in a nightmare I never even remotely expected to be in: my wife and Jake's mother was gone without any notice.

I didn't know you could experience that much hurt and pain. I remember so many times crying so hard, no more sound would come out of my mouth and my eyeballs felt like they would pop out. For several weeks, I couldn't even look at pictures of Lacy without weeping.

Ultimately, I had to make a decision. Do I allow the situation to put me in a pit of pity or do I allow it to fuel a fire that was already burning in me?

I knew this was a direct attack of satan against me and the ministry. We had been advancing in revelation and manifestations. We were seeing miracles everywhere we went — legitimate, doctor verified miracles. The ministry was growing at great speed and we were gaining tremendous momentum.

Satan tried to make me quit, but all he did was make me mad. I was walking through hell, but was determined to keep walking. The great Winston Churchill once said, "When you're going through hell, keep going."

While you are advancing, don't think it strange when the heat gets turned up against you. If satan can't stop you, he will attempt to go after those close to you. Satan will try to do anything he can to stop those who become a threat to his kingdom.

As you begin to advance, you must make a decision every single day: no matter what comes my way, I will not quit. Even if I'm walking through hell, I'll keep walking and while I am walking, I'm going to slay some devils while I am there.

DAY 7
JESUS WAS EXPECTING GREATER

John 5:20 NLT
For the Father loves the Son and shows him everything he is doing. In fact, the Father will show him how to do even greater works than healing this man. Then you will truly be astonished.

Even though Jesus was God in the flesh, Jesus was doing life and ministry as a man anointed by God and in union with God. As a man, Jesus was expecting to advance not only the Kingdom of God, but also advance in revelation.

In John 5:20, Jesus said He was expecting the Father to show Him even greater things...just so Jesus could do them and make everyone say, "Wow!" Isn't that amazing? Not only does this reveal that Jesus was growing in revelation, but it also reveals Jesus was expecting to grow in revelation so He could produce manifestations!

Friend, please understand that if Jesus was expecting to grow in revelation, we should be expecting to grow in revelation. If we as Christians can walk in the love of Jesus, we can also walk in the revelation of Jesus. If we are to be imitators of Christ, shouldn't we imitate His hunger and expectation to advance in the miraculous?

Notice Jesus' statement. This wasn't just an advancement in revelation; this was an advancement in revelation that would produce greater miracles than had been done before!

Now here is my question to you. Is God your Father? If Jesus is your savior and you are born again, then the answer is a resounding, "Yes!" Well, if God is your Father, does He love you? Not only does He love you, but as John 17:24 affirms, God's love for you is as profound as His love for Jesus.

So, if God loves you just like He loves Jesus and if God showed Jesus everything He was doing because He loved Jesus...then that means God will show you all He is doing too. Not only will God show you all He is doing, He will show you even greater things just so you can make the world say, "Wow!"

If Jesus was expecting greater miracles, you should be expecting greater miracles. If you want to advance in the things of God, it is going to require an expectation to hear from God and see from God greater than what you have heard and seen before! It is time to increase your expectation! If the Father would do it for Jesus, He will do it for you!

DAY 8
KNOWING HIS VOICE

John 10:4 NKJV
And when he brings out his own sheep, he goes before them; and the sheep follow him, for they know his voice.

In John 10, Jesus gave us a tremendous teaching in which He compares Himself as the Shepherd and us as His sheep. There is a statement He makes in John 10:4 that is so simple that we unfortunately miss it. Jesus said, "The sheep know His voice."

This needs to be a truth that becomes not just part of our confession, but part of our existence: I know His voice.

When you are born again, God becomes your Father and Jesus becomes your big brother. The Holy Spirit comes to live on the inside of you. You are perfect in God's eyes and filled with Him. God is a spirit and you are a spirit.

In spite of these wonderful truths of which we all embrace as Christians, why do we find it difficult to hear from God? Could it be because we have been told so?

Here is a question for you to ponder: why is it that as a born again Christian, you easily hear from the devil on a daily basis, but struggle hearing from God? How is it possible that you hear demonic temptations but struggle to hear loving promises from your Father?

Why is it when someone needs an answer from God, they need to fast and pray for weeks, but all throughout their day, easily hear the thoughts, ideas, and suggestions of satan?

I would suggest to you that hearing God's voice is not the problem. The problem is we *believe* that hearing from God is hard.

Friend, if you are going to advance in life, it will only happen by hearing His voice and obeying what He says to you. Start changing the way you think about this. Begin saying this on an hourly basis: "I know the voice of God."

Ever since Jake was a newborn, I have put my arms around him every night and prayed over him. Part of my nightly prayer over Jake has been this: "Father, I thank you that Jake knows your voice. He hears from You and sees from You. Hearing from You is normal and natural for him..." It is something I have instilled in him because I have always known this one thing about raising my son: I may not do everything perfect, but if I can teach him to know the voice of God and he obeys what he hears, Jake will be unstoppable in life.

Let this be your new perspective in life and in your fellowship with God. Jesus said it about His sheep, so it must be true. If Jesus is your shepherd, then you know His voice. You will recognize His voice above all of the other voices in the world. Hearing from Him is normal, natural, and easy. His voice is the most recognizable voice in the world to your ears because He is yours and you are His.

DAY 9
WHAT ARE YOU DESIRING

Psalm 20:4 NIV
May he give you the desire of your heart and make all your plans succeed.

If you want to advance, you must have desires to advance. Now listen to what I just said. Not only must you possess the desire to advance, but you must also have aspirations that warrant progression. There must be something in your heart that needs to be advanced before you can advance. This is about vision, my friend. If you don't have vision, you may be moving, but you will only be wandering.

My question for you today is simply this: what do you want? Notice God didn't mention anything about your needs. He didn't say He would give you the needs of your life. Friend, God as your Father is already obligated to take care of your needs. God is wanting you to move beyond asking for your needs - He has that covered. God wants you to ask Him for what you want!

Too many of us are focused on what we need. Need is focused on surviving; wants are based on thriving!

Do you realize that if you will ask God what you want, it will take care of the need? That's right. Wants not only surpass the needs, they encompass the need.

If you are going to ask God for what you want, this means you need to start dreaming. Everyone who advances in any area of life starts with a dream about it. Needs are presented to you by circumstances; wants are presented to you by dreams. My friend, you need to dream if you want to advance.

Notice also that your wants and dreams are tied to your plans. God promised in Psalm 20:4 that He would give you the desires of your heart and make your plans to succeed. I have never met anyone who is focused on their needs that has great plans for their life. Do you know why? It's extremely difficult to develop a five point business plan and implement it if you can barely keep the lights on and food in pantry! Believe me…I understand. I have been there and done that.

I remember for many years of my life that the dreams I had within me were shut away for a long time because every day I was focused on taking care of my needs. I was trying to get enough money to get milk and bread and put a few dollars of gas in my car! My prayers to God were about my needs; however, I found that as I started putting His plans first, my needs began to instantly be taken care of and now I was able to focus on the wants.

God wants to give you your desires so He can make the plans succeed. There is no advancing the plan if there is no want, desire and dream to fuel the plan. Always remember that your wants will get you what you need…plus some.

Don't ask God for what you need; ask God for what you want. I guarantee you this one thing: if you want what you want for the reason *God* wants, you can have all you want. Let God advance your wants and He will advance the plan for your life.

DAY 10
THE POWER OF YOUR IMAGINATION

> *Genesis 11:4-6 KJV*
> *And they said, Go to, let us build us a city and a tower, whose top may reach unto heaven; and let us make us a name, lest we be scattered abroad upon the face of the whole earth. And the Lord came down to see the city and the tower, which the children of men builded. And the Lord said, Behold, the people is one, and they have all one language; and this they begin to do: and now nothing will be restrained from them, which they have imagined to do.*

More than 2,000 years before Jesus was on the earth, the city of Babel was founded by Nimrod, who was Noah's great grandson. At this time, the Babylonian people decided to build a tower to reach up into Heaven. The ancient historian Josephus wrote that Nimrod was determined to build a tower too high for the waters to reach…just in case God decided to flood the earth again.

The Lord came down to see the city and the tower the people of Babel were building. An interesting statement is made by the

Lord in Genesis 11:6 in which He says, "Now nothing will be restrained from them which they have imagined to do."

Usually when we hear about the story of the tower of Babel, it is mostly used in teaching about leadership and they focus on the statement about the people being one. Unity of the team is pretty much the topic talked about when using the tower of Babel as an example. However, I want you to notice something extremely important: the unity of the people was the result of what they had imagined to do.

Many teachings on the Tower of Babel focus on the byproduct, unity, rather than the source, which is imagination. There is much to say in the Bible about the imagination, but interestingly enough, we don't hear much about it in our churches. Imagination is often relegated to children's playful fantasies or dismissed as a source of sinful thoughts and desires.

Do you realize that God is the one who gave us an imagination? God gave us a mind with the ability to reach out and think beyond what is possible. I honestly believe that our imagination is a doorway into the spirit; our imagination allows us to tap into the heart of God.

God recognized that they would accomplish what they had imagined and so He confused their languages; as a result, the people not only stopped working on the tower, but left town and spread out throughout the world.

Our imagination is a powerful thing and something God gave us. Why is it so powerful? Because what you imagine will become your reality. I've said it like this for years and will continue saying it because it is true: whatever has your imagination has your faith.

Friend, let me let you in on a secret: we don't have a faith problem; we have an imagination problem. Your faith works! You have the faith of God. If you have the love, peace, joy, self-control of God... then you also possess His faith, which is always fruitful.

We need to harness our imagination and allow ourselves to start meditating, pondering and imagining once again. It's not wasted time to envision God's promises manifesting in your life. Using your imagination to picture yourself fulfilling God's plan for your life is a productive endeavor.

God gave you an imagination to use for His glory, not for the devil's schemes. But this is why satan brings thoughts, ideas, and suggestions your way - he wants you to imagine the curse at work in your life. It is what he did to Eve and what he wants to do with you. Do you know why? Because he understands that the object of your imagination fuels your faith, and your faith brings forth your reality.

If you want to advance in the things of God and advance in His plan for your life, I am telling you now: it will never happen without a godly imagination that is free to roam and dream without religious fences.

Imagination will transport you from the realm of impossibilities to the realm of possibilities. Imagination will move you from mere religious practice to a dynamic relationship with God—one that nurtures desires and dreams, kindling the passion in your heart to further His Kingdom.

DAY 11
INSIDER SECRETS

1 Corinthians 14:2 AMP
For one who speaks in an unknown tongue does not speak to people but to God; for no one understands him or catches his meaning, but by the Spirit he speaks mysteries [secret truths, hidden things].

One of the supernatural tools God has given us to help us in advancing in life is the ability to pray/speak in other tongues. This may be a foreign concept to you — if it is, you need to make it common. Praying in tongues is only weird because people have made it weird. If you keep it Scriptural, there is nothing weird about it.

In 1 Corinthians 14, the apostle Paul gives us some wonderful benefits to praying tongues — one of those being the fact that we can pray out the secrets of God. Did you know God has secrets? That's right! God has secrets that He wants to let you in on! He is not hiding things from you; He is hiding them for you and speaking in tongues is one of the ways we access them.

When we pray in tongues, the Holy Spirit is giving us the words and helping us to pray the hidden, secret things of God. When we pray in tongues, we pray perfect prayers; we pray out the perfect will of God; we pray out secrets.

As we are advancing in the things of God, advancing in revelation and advancing in His plan, there will be questions that arise. The answers to some of these questions will not be available in the natural realm because it will require supernatural wisdom. There have been many times where I had an important decision and I didn't know what to do or even how to pray about it. So do you know what I did? I began praying in tongues. I said, "Holy Spirit, help me to pray out the solution to this problem" and I would begin to pray in tongues.

Now, you might ask, "How does this help if you don't understand what you are saying?" That's a great question. The answer is simple: I pray by faith. The apostle Paul goes on to say in 1 Corinthians 14:13 that we are to pray for the interpretation as well. So as I am praying, I am also believing for the understanding of what I am praying. Now, it may not be immediate — sometimes it is and sometimes it may be a day or two or even a few weeks later — but all of a sudden, it is like a thought hits my head and I know exactly what I need to do.

Not only does praying in tongues help us get answers, it also opens the door to insider secrets. In the business world, you see people make huge advances in the financial arena because of having inside information. What if you could have that in every area of your life? Well, you can by spending time praying in tongues. The Holy Spirit is a genius and He knows all things that are pertinent to your success and advancement in life.

We must go for greater and go beyond what is available in the natural. If we are going to manifest the Kingdom of God and fulfill the original commission of filling and subduing the earth, we must tap into the deep, secret, and hidden things of God by praying in other tongues. This is why it is important that we spend time every day praying in tongues with the intent of hearing from God. Just like one can speak in their native tongue, we can also speak in another tongue that our mind doesn't understand, but our spirit does by the Holy Spirit.

As we advance in our prayer language, we will advance in our walk with God and ultimately advance the Kingdom of God.

DAY 12
GROW BEYOND YOUR SENSES

Hebrews 12:9 NKJV
Furthermore, we have had human fathers who corrected us, and we paid them respect. Shall we not much more readily be in subjection to the Father of spirits and live?

If God is the Father of spirits and God is your Father, then what does that make you? That's right — it makes you a spirit. This is also what we learn from Genesis 1:26 in which God said, "Let's make man in our image, according to our likeness." God made us as spirit beings. This is a truth revealed all throughout the Bible and yet, sadly, it is a truth a majority of the Church has failed to grasp.

Being a spirit is part of your identity; it is who you are. You don't have a spirit — you are a spirit. If you are a spirit, then we should be sensitive to spiritual things because we have spiritual senses. In the same way we have physical senses, we have spiritual senses. How do we know this?

Jesus tells a story in Luke 16 about a man who had died and went to hell. He sees across the chasm over into Paradise and begins to talk to Abraham. In this story, the man is seeing and hearing Abraham. The man states that he is thirsty and hot because of the flames. He then goes on to talk about his brothers on the earth and his concern about their salvation.

In this story, you have a man who has died (or you could say a spirit who has left their body) and you see him using all five senses as well remembering his family on earth. You don't get spiritual senses when you die; you have them the entire time you are on the earth. Do you know why? Because you are a spirit.

When you were born into this earth, you came into this earth as a spirit in a body. As a result, we should be just as sensitive to spiritual things as we are physical things. Why are we not? Because we have grown up in a world dominated by the flesh and raised in homes in which there is no emphasis on spiritual things.

Sadly, there are people who operate in the occult who are far more sensitive to spiritual things than ministers in the churches. The reason why is simple: they have been intentional in growing beyond their senses.

How do we grow beyond our senses? We do so by first recognizing we are a spirit. Second, we must renew our mind to the reality that the spirit realm is just as real as the natural realm. Third, we must be intentional about controlling our thoughts and emotions so that our soul is not in control. Fourth, we must spend time in the Word and praying in the Spirit. Finally, we must spend time getting quiet, meditating on spiritual things, and intentionally become more conscious of the spirit realm.

As we begin to grow beyond our senses, we will begin to advance further in the things of God than any man or woman in Christ has ever been. In the natural, there are limits to how far you can advance; however, in the spirit, there are no boundaries.

DAY 13
CONTROL YOUR TEMPER

Ephesians 4:26-27 NLT
And "don't sin by letting anger control you." Don't let the sun go down while you are still angry, for anger gives a foothold to the devil.

I used to work in the prison system and I saw so many men that were in prison simply because they chose not to control their emotions. I have heard it so many times over the years, "I just can't control my temper." Well, that is simply an excuse that carries no truth. You can control your temper because you choose how you are going to respond to a situation.

Controlling your temper may not sound very spiritual, but if you want to advance in life, you will have to put your anger on a leash. Do you know why? Because your out-of-control anger will open doors for satan to operate in your life.

I will be the first to admit...growing up, I had a temper. I have had to work on it over the years because it didn't take much for me to blow up. As I began to tame it, I got to the point where I became very patient in dealing with people; however, it was still a problem when you pushed me past the edge of my patience — because then I would still blow up.

Now understand: there is nothing wrong with being angry. Actually, being angry is not a sin. There is a thing the Bible refers to as "righteous anger." We see this take place with Jesus when He went into the temple with a whip and drove out all the moneychangers (John 2:15). Jesus got mad to the point He actually took the time to make a whip and then went after them!

Notice Ephesians 4 says "don't sin by letting anger control you." The Bible doesn't say that anger is a sin; it says it is a sin by letting it control you. I am very thankful that the Holy Spirit tells us in 2 Timothy 1:7 that we have been given a spirit of love, power and of self-control. This tells us that we have the self control of God! Just because someone cuts you off on the highway does not mean you have to get road rage and start tailgating them!

This is crucial if you want to advance in your relationships. If you want to keep getting stronger in your marriage or your relationship with your children, you need to be in control of your temper. I know many marriages that have been destroyed because one of the spouses, usually the husband, couldn't control their temper.

Friend, if you want to advance, if you want to go after greater, you need to have some soul control — which includes controlling your anger. You don't want anything controlling you in life, especially your temper. When you don't control your temper, your temper controls you and thus, satan begins to control you. The result: you stop advancing.

DAY 14
GUARD YOUR DREAM

Matthew 7:6 NKJV
Do not give what is holy to the dogs; nor cast your pearls before swine, lest they trample them under their feet, and turn and tear you in pieces.

Every one of us has a dream that needs to be fulfilled, but in order to fulfill it, we must protect it. Jesus gave us a tremendous nugget of wisdom in Matthew 7 in which He said, "Don't cast your pearls before swine." One of those pearls you need to protect is your dream. Not everyone needs to hear your dream — especially those who will trample on it.

When God gives you a dream that He needs you to advance, one of the wisest things you can do is to guard it and meditate on it. One of the most foolish things you can do with your dream is to immediately announce it to the world.

One great example of this in the Bible is found in the story of Joseph in Genesis 37. Joseph was given dreams to reveal things about his future. Instead of keeping them to himself, he told those dreams to his family and it led to years of hell. His brothers despised him so much, they dug a pit, threw Joseph in it and left him for dead.

Because of the "kindness" of one brother, they decided to pull Joseph out of the pit and sell him as a slave. Joseph eventually ends up serving in Potiphar's house — only to be accused of rape and then thrown in prison. Eventually, because of the favor of God, Joseph interprets a dream for Pharaoh and is promoted to second in command of Egypt.

It's a wild story of how Joseph became the prince of Egypt, but I have often wondered, "Did Joseph really have to be left for dead, become a slave, be accused of rape and thrown in prison…just so God could get him before Pharaoh?" Most people say this entire process was the plan of God, but I'm not so sure about that.

What would have happened if he would have just put the dream on the shelf of his mind, meditated, prayed about it and allowed God to bring it to pass? Yes, God is sovereign and can fulfill His plans however He chooses; however, I firmly believe if Joseph had been wise about the revealing of his dreams, he wouldn't have had to go through all of that torment in order for those dreams to come to pass.

Isn't it interesting that Jesus didn't go around telling everyone everything that God had put in His heart? How many times would Jesus tell people not to reveal who He was or not to tell what had happened? There was wisdom and purpose in this so that Jesus would not have unnecessary hindrances to fulfilling the plan of God.

Just because God has shown you something for your future, it doesn't mean you need to just start blabbing it to all those around you. God wants you to go for greater and that is why He will give you thoughts, ideas and insight into your future. He will give you glimpses and knowings of the things He has for you, but you would be a fool to just start going out and telling everyone.

Advancing requires wisdom in protecting the dream God has given you. The dream of God for your life is precious and must be protected because satan will do anything and everything he can to stop it - even by having those you love stomp on the dream because their vision is too small for themselves and for you. The best thing you can do is keep your dreams away from the pigs and keep them between you and God until He shows you it is time for it to be revealed.

DAY 15
THEY ARE CHEERING FOR YOU

Hebrews 12:2 NKJV
Therefore we also, since we are surrounded by so great a cloud of witnesses, let us lay aside every weight, and the sin which so easily ensnares us, and let us run with endurance the race that is set before us.

Have you ever heard of home field advantage? There is something to be said about being a sports team and getting to play at home. Do you know why? It's the fans in the stadium. Things may look different from stadium to stadium but there is no real advantage because both teams are playing in the same conditions. The major difference is the people in the stands. If you are at home, they are cheering for you. If you are away, they are booing you.

Now if you are like me, I loved going into opposing teams' stadiums. I didn't mind hearing the boos; they only motivated me to play even harder. I loved to go in and beat our opponents in front of their own crowd in their home gym (there has always been a little bit of a rebel in me). However, there is a real reason that teams fight hard to win during the regular season and it is because there is the advantage of getting to play your playoff games at home instead of on the road.

Hebrews 12:2 tells us that we are surrounded by a great cloud of witnesses. These are people that have finished their race on the earth and have gone before us to Heaven. We all have at least someone that we cared about that has already gone to Heaven. You may be missing them, but let me give you some motivation: they are one of the millions of witnesses watching your race.

Now I remember growing up playing sports in which there would be hundreds, if not thousands in the stands. Even though there were lots of people cheering, there was something special about knowing your loved ones were in the stands cheering for you. There was always a little bit more motivation for me to play harder when I knew my close friends or family were watching. Well my friend, I want you to know that your loved ones that have gone before you, they are watching your race and they are cheering you on.

You see, to be a witness, you have to witness something. They may not be privy to the clothes you are wearing or the car you are driving, but they are very much aware of your spiritual advancement of the things of God. I don't know if it is on a massive version of a spiritual LED screen in Heaven, whether it is announced on a loudspeaker, or if there is just a Holy Spirit revealed knowing…but they know of your spiritual progress.

I've always been extremely motivated in what I set out to do and accomplish and especially regarding the call of God on my life. When Lacy moved to Heaven, it even further motivated me to push even harder and to advance even further. Why? Because we started the ministry together and I had a job to finish. And do you know what? It gives me great motivation to know that she and many others are cheering me on.

This should give you great solace as well when you are pushing through the tough times and you feel all alone. Believe me, I know exactly what it feels like to be doing good things, remaining faithful and going through hard times while it seems no one even knows what you are accomplishing.

Friend, always know that what you are doing for the Kingdom of God is being noticed. There may not be millions on the earth cheering for you, but there are hundreds of millions cheering for you in Heaven.

Every morning, I want you to wake up and imagine the millions and millions of people chanting your name, encouraging you to keep going, encouraging you not to quit, and telling you, "Good job!" Know that God is always with you. God has never left you or forsaken you. Not only is God watching, but all of Heaven is on your side cheering you on while you advance.

DAY 16
NO MORE EXCUSES

> *Genesis 3:11-13 NLT*
> *"Who told you that you were naked?" the Lord God asked. "Have you eaten from the tree whose fruit I commanded you not to eat?" The man replied, "It was the woman you gave me who gave me the fruit, and I ate it." Then the Lord God asked the woman, "What have you done?" "The serpent deceived me," she replied. "That's why I ate it."*

One thing that irritates the fire out of me is excuses. I hate excuses. Either put up or shut up, but don't make excuses. Own your mistakes, own your lack of gumption, own your lack of desire to advance…but don't make excuses for it.

In Genesis 3:11, God confronts Adam about eating from the tree of good and evil. Satan had deceived Eve into eating of the fruit; but do you know who was really to blame? It was all Adam's fault. Now you would think that Adam would be apologetic! Adam went from walking in the glory of God to immediately becoming spiritually dead and physically naked! Instead of

Adam falling to his knees in repentance, do you know what Adam said? Adam's response to God was, "That woman you gave me, she gave me the fruit." Then God looks to Eve and says, "Why did you do this?" Was Eve repentant? Would she end up being the bigger person? Nope! Eve said, "It was the snake's fault!" God looked at the serpent and the serpent didn't have anyone else to blame! It was one excuse after another.

Sadly, I often hear excuses for our lack of advancement from many in the Church. The world doesn't put up with excuses; you provide excuses, you get fired. In the Church, we get excuses and find Scripture for them so as to make ourselves feel better and not have to push forward.

I refuse to make excuses when Jesus has not only provided the way, but also told us it is possible to go after greater. I refuse to make excuses for my lack of advancement and I refuse to make excuses for my mistakes. When you do make a mistake, you need to own up to it; whether it is with your parents, boss, friend, coworkers or even God.

Own your mistake. Do you know why? Because if you don't own your mistake, your mistake will own you. Instead of learning from your mistake and growing from it, that excuse will keep you right where you are at and you will not advance.

DAY 17
GO FOR GREATER

John 14:12 ESV
...whoever believes in me will also do the works that I do; and greater works than these will he do, because I am going to the Father.

One day, Jesus looked at His disciples and said, "Whoever believes in me can do what I did and even greater!" That's an astounding statement when you look at all of the miracles Jesus accomplished. Let's break this statement down a bit.

Jesus said, "Whoever believes in Me..." This promise was not to the person who stands behind a pulpit. This promise was not to a graduate of a Bible school or someone in full time ministry. This promise was to the believer. Are you a "whoever?" If you are a believer in Jesus, you qualify. What do you qualify for? You qualify for the promise Jesus made: "Whoever believes in me will do the same works..." What are the "same works?" Every time Jesus mentioned "doing the works," He was always referring to miracles.

Jesus then goes on to say that those who believe in Him would do greater works! Jesus revealed that what He did on the earth was to be the floor, not the ceiling for the works of the Church. Think about what I just said. We have looked at the works of Jesus and acted like that was the limit of what could be achieved - but this is not true based on the statement of Jesus. Jesus expected us to do greater.

Now I have heard all of the excuses from very intelligent theologians; they are intelligent, but dumb because instead of taking Jesus at His word, they try to explain away what Jesus said. Jesus was extremely clear, "Whoever believes in me will do the same and even greater works because I am going to the Father."

Jesus expected increase from the Church. Jesus expected that His seating at the right hand of God would be the launching of the Church into an advancement of Himself in the world. Jesus fully expected His Church, His body to partake of all authority in Heaven and on earth, their union with Christ and blow past what Jesus did on the earth with a lesser authority and operating under a lesser covenant.

For those that think it is not possible to do greater than what Jesus did on the earth, the only option is to believe that Jesus is dead. No, Jesus is alive and He is alive in us! He is the head and we are the body! We are the hands and feet of Jesus! Jesus can certainly work through us and outdo what He has done before.

So what is stopping us from advancing in this area? Our perspective. We must start seeing ourselves for who we truly are - one with Christ. This is about identity and knowing our position in Him. The more you begin to believe what Jesus said, the more you will begin to experience what He said.

DAY 18
GET OUT OF ELEMENTARY SCHOOL

Hebrews 6:1-3 NKJV
Therefore, leaving the discussion of the elementary principles of Christ, let us go on to perfection, not laying again the foundation of repentance from dead works and of faith toward God, of the doctrine of baptisms, of laying on of hands, of resurrection of the dead, and of eternal judgment. And this we will do if God permits.

Over the last two thousand years, the Church has grown in number, but unfortunately, we have not grown in revelation to the degree that we should have grown. Some would argue with that statement, but look at Hebrews 6:1-3 and you will see it proves we have not really grown like we should.

Look at the subjects that are listed and considered to be "baby" stuff: repentance, faith, baptism, laying on of hands, resurrection, and judgment. Now, think about what has been preached on over the last hundred years and tell me this: why are we still in elementary school?

Can you imagine walking into a first grade class and seeing a student that is thirty years old? We know there would be something terribly wrong with that picture. Do you realize that as absurd as that scenario is, we have that in our churches every Sunday? We have hundreds of millions of Christians all around the world who are still attending the elementary school of God even though they have been saved for decades.

Even the apostle Paul said that we need to push for more! He said we need to move on to perfection. Even in Colossians 1:28, the apostle Paul said, "Him we preach, warning every man and teaching every man in all wisdom, that we may present every man perfect in Christ Jesus." Do you realize what has just been said? You can't reach perfection if you are still in elementary school!

You wouldn't settle for lack of personal progress in school, so why would you do that in the things of God? Stop settling and start advancing in revelation. Realize there is more available. Be determined to move beyond elementary school, go to middle school and graduate high school. Be one of the first of your generation to go on to the higher studies of Christ. It's time to advance and get your diploma!

DAY 19
EMBRACE WISDOM

Proverbs 4:7-8 NKJV
Wisdom is the principal thing; Therefore get wisdom. And in all your getting, get understanding. Exalt her, and she will promote you; She will bring you honor, when you embrace her.

In the day and age that we live in, there is a wealth of information at our fingertips. You can simply pick up your phone and do an internet search of any subject you would like. You can now even speak to some internet connected devices and ask how to complete a certain task. Despite all of the information available to us, nothing can compare to the wisdom of God's Word.

Solomon, who at his time was the wisest man in the world, said the following: "Exalt wisdom and she will promote you. She will bring you honor when you embrace her." Because we have grown up in a cursed world in which the cultures and societies are against the realities of God, it becomes easy to look to the wisdom of the world. The wisdom of the world will tell you that at a particular time is the time to sell your stocks, but is that the wisdom of God? The wisdom of the world will tell you a vaccine is the answer to a particular disease, but is that the wisdom of God?

In every area of life, the world has its wisdom, but God also has His. Friend, when the wisdom of the world goes contrary to the wisdom of God, I go with the wisdom of God every time — regardless of what it costs me in the world.

You will find that the wisdom of the world is constantly changing but God's Word never changes. God's wisdom is dependable, trustworthy and if you will embrace it, you will be exalted. If you will listen and follow His Word, you will look like a genius. If you will embrace God's wisdom, success and favor will embrace you.

No matter what you are going through, no matter what circumstance you are facing, you can find the wisdom of God in His written Word. Not only that, the Holy Spirit is your Teacher and the Revealer of all truth. In the specific areas of life, such as who to marry, what house to buy, what job to take, etc., the Holy Spirit will give you wisdom to make the right decision at the right time.

If you get His wisdom, nothing can stop you from advancing.

DAY 20
WORK FOR THE LORD

Colossians 3:23-24 NLT
Work willingly at whatever you do, as though you were working for the Lord rather than for people. Remember that the Lord will give you an inheritance as your reward, and that the Master you are serving is Christ.

Most people are going to work a job for several decades and most are always going to have a boss. If you want to advance in a supernatural way, you need to have the right attitude when it comes to work. What is that attitude? It is simple: "whatever I do, I am working for God."

Colossians 3:23 says we are to work willingly at whatever we do as unto the Lord. This isn't talking only about a ministry job or at your volunteer job at church - this is about any job! Whether it is a job at a ministry or a job at a department store, a job with a mean boss or a job with a nice boss - we are to work as unto the Lord.

If you want to advance in your job, this is one major way you can do it. Look at even the most menial tasks at your job and act like you were doing it for Jesus. Do it willingly and give it your best.

Not only are there earthly rewards for working hard and doing what is right, do you realize there is a Heavenly reward for simply going to your job and working like you are working for Jesus? Colossians 3 tells us so! Because you work willingly at your job for the Lord, there is an eternal inheritance.

So many times, we go through life with an earthly mindset, but we need to have an eternal mindset as well. We are not just living for now; we are also living for the future. Your attitude at work will not only bring you advancement on the earth; it will bring you advancement in Heaven!

DAY 21
EVERYTHING IS POSSIBLE

Matthew 19:26 NLT
Jesus looked at them intently and said, "Humanly speaking, it is impossible. But with God everything is possible."

As we advance, we will encounter some seemingly impossible situations; in these times, we must know that everything is possible with God. A large part of my ministry has been focused in the area of healing. In dealing with physical situations over the last twenty years, there hasn't been much that has made me take a step back and say, "This is impossible." I have studied and meditated so much in the area of healing, I know beyond a shadow of a doubt that even though it looks impossible, it actually is possible.

I have also encountered financial situations in which it looked impossible. Growing up in poverty, this was an area that I really had to work on; however, as I continued to grow in my understanding of God's promises in the area of money, I have seen time and time again the faithfulness of God in the financial arena of taking impossible situations and God making them possible.

Despite seeing physical and financial miracles on a regular basis for the last twenty years, there was one situation I was presented with in which, I am embarrassed to admit, but I called it impossible. When my first wife Lacy passed away, I was brokenhearted, devastated and numb. I was forty-six years old with a fourteen year old son to raise on my own. Our ministry was growing and I had an extremely busy travel schedule. We were having the best time of our lives and ministry and all of a sudden, it was shattered.

Over the process of time, loneliness and the reality of doing life alone as a single dad was really setting in. I remember in one of my study times, I thought about the possibility of getting married again and I wrote down a list of some "must haves" in a wife. Because of Jake, the ministry and my particular focus in ministry, there were some qualities that would be needed that I refused to compromise on. A few of those that I wrote down were: ministry minded, same beliefs in healing, widow and brunette.

I obviously wrote ministry minded and same beliefs because the ministry is my life and I needed a partner that had the same vision as me. I wrote down widow because I wanted to have someone in my life that had gone through the same situation as me and Jake, that understood our feelings and emotions, but also would allow Jake to talk freely about Lacy without any jealousy. I also wrote down brunette. It may seem odd, but Lacy was a platinum blonde and I just couldn't, for myself or for Jake, have another woman in our home that would be any type of trigger for us.

As I looked at this list, I realized this was an impossible list. After all, I only had a few guy friends that believe exactly what I believe! I hate admitting this, but this list looked so impossible to me, I didn't even bother asking God. I looked at that list and realized I was going to be alone for the rest of my life because I would not compromise for Jake and I would not compromise for the ministry. Admittedly, I sat there and cried a bit, but I sucked it up and determined I would push through like a good soldier.

Well, one day I got a call from one of my best friends. He asked me to come to Birmingham, Alabama and pray for one of his close friends who had been diagnosed with cancer; I also found out it was one of my ministry partners. So I flew to Birmingham, met my friend and we went to Grand View Medical Center.

As we walked into room 914, standing to the front of my partner's bed was her cousin named April. April was a beautiful brunette that was forty-one years old, a widow, and formerly involved in ministry. Needless to say, I had a hard time focusing on my ministry partner. I was trying to contain my emotions because this "impossible list" was standing beside me in the flesh.

Later that night, we talked on the phone and she began to tell me about her heart for the healing ministry. Jake was asleep in my bedroom and I remember walking into my bathroom, dropping to the floor and my emotions just flooded out of me. I told God, "God, if this is a joke, this isn't funny!" Did God truly send Jake and me the impossible? I sat on the bathroom floor feeling convicted that I had doubted God but also elated because, once again, God had shown that 'God was good to Chad.'

Long story short, April and I got married several months later. I watched God take an impossible situation and in only a way that God could do, He took two families who had experienced great tragedy, brought them together, and blended them seamlessly. When people ask April about what God did for us, her response is short and yet perfect, "But God." It seemed impossible… but God.

Friend, I want to encourage you today. Whatever impossible situation you are facing, I want you to know it's possible. Whether it is physical, financial or relational, there is nothing impossible with God. He can pay an impossible bill, He can heal an impossible disease and He can also bring you the impossible person.

DAY 22
WHATEVER YOU SAY

Luke 1:38 NKJV
Then Mary said, "Behold the maidservant of the Lord! Let it be to me according to your word." And the angel departed from her.

I have always admired Mary, the mother of Jesus, because of one tremendous decision that she made. One day an angel appeared to her and revealed that she was to be the mother of the Messiah. Now it is important to not forget that at this time of the angel's appearance, not only is Mary a young Jewish teenager, she is also engaged to be married. In making this decision to become pregnant by the seed of the Lord, she faced a natural situation in which (1) her soon to be husband would leave her but (2) she could be stoned for being pregnant and out of wedlock. Despite the potential consequences, Mary made a powerful statement, "Lord, let it be to me according to your word." In other words, "God, whatever you say, I will do it."

Have you been in a situation that God asked you to do something, but it seemed impossible or by doing so, it could potentially bring problems in the natural? If you are advancing, you will be in this type of situation over and over. As you are advancing in the things of God and advancing in your calling, I guarantee that God is going to ask you to do some seemingly impossible things. In those times, this is where you take the step of faith and say, "God, whatever you say."

I remember our very first year of pastoring, we had outgrown our small rented building and I was looking for something bigger. I decided I didn't want to rent anything; I wanted to own a building. I went to God about it and do you know what He told me to do? Sow $10,000 to another ministry! Those who know me know that I love to give and I would have gladly given it at that time, but do you know what my problem was? We only had $500 in our bank account.

That next Sunday, I stood before our church and told them the Lord had told us to sow $10,000 to this particular ministry as a seed for our building and that whatever came in the offering was going towards that seed. That day, the people of our church gave $4500; so, that gave us $5,000 of what was needed. Two days later, I went to the post office and guess what was in the mail? It was a check for $5,000 from another church that had no clue as to what we were doing. I remember being twenty-nine years old, nine months into full time ministry and realizing what God had just done. He told me to give $10,000 and we didn't have it — but within three days, He gave us the seed that He wanted us to sow.

The next day, I wrote out a check for $10,000 to this ministry. I remember trembling with excitement because (1) I had never written a check for that much and (2) I was so excited at what God had done!

A few weeks later, I found an old dilapidated building in the downtown area for rent and I knew I was supposed to sign a lease on it for our church. It was disgusting but I knew it was God. So I said, "God, whatever you say!" and I signed a five year lease, with the first right of refusal and signed as the personal guarantor on it. Now mind you, this was a 10,000 sq ft building that was full of asbestos and needed a complete renovation and I am talking about down to the steel beams and concrete slab. It was going to be close to one million dollars to get this building usable - and don't forget that we had just given all of our money away!

Friend, I will never forget looking at that building and wondering, "Where is the money going to come from to fix this?" I was twenty-nine years old with no construction experience and I personally was flat broke and our church had a few hundred dollars in the bank account. But guess what happened? I got a phone call from a representative from the mayor's office. They said, "Would you be willing to meet us for lunch? We would like to discuss a potential purchase of your lease for the building downtown." Well, that certainly got my curiosity!

The next day, I met two city representatives at Applebee's on the corner of Texas Avenue and University Boulevard in College Station, TX. They told me the city was in the process of renovating the entire city center. They had a list of twenty properties they needed to purchase for the new development and they had purchased all of the properties but one. Guess which property they needed to purchase? You got it: the one I had just signed the lease on.

After a few city council meetings, I got called to the mayor's office. The scene was like something out of a movie. I walked into a big room with men in suits as they slid an upside down piece of paper across the table. One man said, "Chad, here is our offer to buy you out of your lease." It was a check for $100,000! Do you know what I did? I signed off on it! And do you know what happened? We were also given the opportunity to purchase a 1.2 million dollar building for the purchase price of $550,000 with nothing down and for it to be owner financed.

In a few short months, our new church of seventy people went from having $500 in our bank account and meeting in a vacant restaurant to having $100,000 in our bank account and purchasing a 1.2 million dollar building with no down payment. All it took was saying, "God, whatever you say."

DAY 23
GO TO THE PLACE I WILL SHOW YOU

Genesis 12:1 NKJV
Now the Lord had said to Abram: "Get out of your country, from your family and from your father's house, to a land that I will show you."

Several years ago, I was faced with a decision that could have had horrible repercussions if it went wrong. I had been sensing it was time to start putting my full focus on the healing ministry—which meant I needed to step down from my pastoral position of the church and begin traveling full time. Many people look at where things are at presently and would think that decision was not a big deal, but it was a huge deal because I didn't have ministry partners and I had no schedule. I had people say I was just going to greener pastures. Friend, there was nothing on the other side of the fence but a ditch!

On top of that, I had made a decision that if this was what God was calling me to do, there were three things I was not going to do: (1) I would never ask for meetings from pastors (2) I would never make any financial demands and (3) I would cover all of my travel costs. As you can see, the odds were already stacked against me!

I knew it was the right thing to do; so we stepped down from our position as the senior pastors of the church and moved to Oklahoma. Do you know what happened a few months later? Covid showed up and all travel was shut down and most churches closed. Now, can you imagine what was going through my mind at that point? I had one meeting for the entire year, a handful of partners and no income - and here I was starting a traveling ministry focused on healing in the middle of a worldwide pandemic…and not asking for meetings.

One Sunday morning, I had an older gentleman come up to me at the end of the service. He said, "Chad, I have a word from the Lord for you. The Lord showed me that its like you have been flying at 50,000 feet for several years. During this time, God has been showing you things other people haven't seen, but He is about to create a runway for you to land on and tell the world about these hidden things of God."

Now I will be honest, when a stranger comes up to me and says they have a "word" from the Lord for me, I take it with a great deal of skepticism. However, there was something different about this situation: it bore witness with me. I had never met this man before, but I knew God was up to something.

A few weeks later, I received a call from a major Christian television ministry and from that, the ministry doors blew open. The letters and emails from pastors and new partners started coming in.

By the end of 2020, we ended up having our best year ministerially and financially we had ever had. Do you know what happened in 2021? We doubled what we did in 2020! Do you know what has happened every year since then? We have doubled in number every year! Friends, that is the faithfulness of God!

Friend, advancing requires taking steps of faith and sometimes going to a place God will show you...when you get there. You don't need to have everything planned out. Certainly there is wisdom in planning, but there will be times that God tells you to skip the planning and just go — and when He says go, you just go knowing that His provision is in the going.

Never in my wildest dreams did I think I would end up where I am, but I am so thankful I went not knowing where I was going, just knowing that God said, "Go."

DAY 24
PUT YOUR FOCUS ON OTHERS

Philippians 2:4 NKJV
Let each of you look out not only for his own interests,
but also for the interests of others.

It is easy to get to a place of settling when you are only focused on yourself. When things are going good for you, there is a tendency to stop pushing; however, when you realize that what you are doing is for the greater good of others, it will push you to go further.

Over the years, I have received criticism from people, especially ministers, as I have continued to push for greater. I have never been one to settle for average. When it comes to your life calling, why would you not continually push the boundaries when you know there is more available?

In the area of healing, I get criticized royally for my stance and my teaching; however, it is easy to criticize when it doesn't affect you on a day to day basis. I have people travel from great distances to my meetings in search of hope and a cure for their physical ailments. Although I am not the healer, I put tremendous pressure on myself to advance, increase, and multiply in my understanding and results in the area of healing. Why do I put this pressure on myself? For two reasons: (1) people's physical lives are on the line and (2) people's spiritual lives are on the line.

When we look at the current state of the body of Christ and compare it to the realities we see in the Word, it's glaringly obvious we have work to do in getting our results up to the standard of Jesus Christ. How does it happen? We humble ourselves and recognize where we are at and then push for more revelation and understanding so that we can help people.

I push everyday for continued insight and advancement in the things of God. There are people I haven't met yet who are counting on me to get to a place of understanding so that they can experience the freedom that only Jesus can give.

The world needs me to advance and they need you to advance. Whatever God has called you to, you need to push past what seems impossible for the world. People you have never met are counting on you to not quit, keep going and push past the impossible.

The world is depending on you to advance so that they can be truly free.

DAY 25
THE CRITICISM OF CRITICS

Proverbs 29:25 GNT
It is dangerous to be concerned with what others think of you, but if you trust the Lord, you are safe.

Over the years, I have had my fair share of critics, but those critics didn't come out until I started down a new, narrow road - a road of advancing. I have found that when you are on the wide road, that is the popular road full of cheerleaders — it is a road that doesn't lead to growth, but simply designed to make you pull over and enjoy the scenery. As soon as you start endeavoring to create a new road, the critics will be in the ditches to tell you how you are wrong.

People's words do not move me. Do you know what moves me? What moves me and keeps me advancing is to finish the work of what Jesus has called me to do. As you advance, you will have critics. No student is above His master; if Jesus had critics, you will have critics too. Jesus had an abundance of critics, but none were worse than the Pharisees.

The Pharisees were the religious leaders of the day. They knew all of the Old Testament scriptures but they were so intelligent with it, they stripped it of its power. They would be those that could teach videos about a subject, write books about the subject, lecture on the subject, tell you the history of the subject and yet be satisfied with producing no fruit on the subject. Not only were they extremely intellectual, they were also extremely critical.

Now friend, I've got bad news for you: we still have Pharisees today. They certainly have more revelation than those in Jesus' day, but they are still here today to be your greatest critic. I am telling you right now, you better get ready for the critics. A lot of people don't like it when you push for more. Do you know why? Because it exposes their lack of desire to increase and/or exposes their inefficiencies. Pharisees love talking, but don't care about producing.

Some of the greatest critics will be those who sit behind their phone and computers. They will bash you on social media and send hateful emails. Do you know what I do? I don't look at them. When I get on social media, I get on to post something and then I turn it off. I don't allow myself to get caught up in the opinions of those who aren't doing anything but criticizing progress.

If you are being moved by your critics, you are not moving towards the plan of God for your life. The critics will kill you if you allow it; instead, base your worth and identity in Christ. Put your sole focus on the voice of one person: Jesus. If you will focus on pleasing Him, you will always be advancing.

DAY 26
THE PRAISES OF MEN

Proverbs 22:4 NLT
True humility and fear of the Lord lead to riches, honor, and long life

As we advance, not only will you receive criticism, you will also receive praise. We all can use a good pat on the back and to hear, "Good job" every once in a while. Where we get into dangerous ground is when we continue to hear "You are amazing" and then begin to think that we are something special.

Proverbs 22:4 tells us that humility will lead you to some good things. In reality, humility will lead you forward, but pride will not only take you backward, it will take you down. In our social media driven world, everyone is after likes, shares and follows. People today actually find their self worth in how many views they get on a video or followers or likes they got on a social media post. Friend, don't fall for the deception. There is nothing wrong with people liking you, appreciating you and following you - just don't let it change you.

We find in the Bible that the Pharisees not only were Jesus' worst critics, but they were also huge hypocrites. Some of them actually believed in Jesus, but they didn't want to publicly acknowledge Him and follow Him because they loved the praises of men more than God (John 12:42-43).

Because of the ministry Jesus called us to, we put a major focus on healing. As a result of the Word that has been preached and our boldness to advance in it, we have seen crazy miracles over the years. So many times, after someone is healed, the crowd will begin to clap and in that moment is when I immediately say, "Let's lift our hands and worship Jesus." I refuse to allow even one moment of an opportunity for people to give me praise or will I allow even a thought to stay in my mind of "Wow! Look at what you did." I will not bow to pride because I recognize that (1) I am not the healer and (2) I am nothing without Jesus.

As we continue to advance, keep your eyes on Jesus. Always give Jesus the praise for what you do and what is accomplished. There is nothing wrong with people thanking you and showing you their gratitude. We certainly are to give honor to whom honor is due — just check your heart when honor is given. Pride always leads to a fall regardless of who you are and what you have accomplished.

DAY 27
BE THANKFUL

Colossians 3:15 NKJV
And let the peace of God rule in your hearts, to which also you were called in one body; and be thankful.

I am extremely goal oriented. I have things I want to accomplish and timelines in which I want to accomplish them. Having this type of drive and mindset, it can lead to disappointment if you don't keep things in the proper perspective.

Whether it is business, athletics or ministry, human nature is always going to bring a little bit of competition. Now there shouldn't be competition in ministry, but nonetheless, it happens when we don't control our thought life. There are comparisons of buildings, followers, book sales, attendance… and if you don't watch it, the comparisons will lead to cares. All of a sudden, your motivation will switch from people to numbers.

When you start focusing more on your image than the mission, you will immediately begin to lose your peace. You will take on the care of comparison instead of the care of the call. Do you know one way you can protect your peace and protect your motivation? Be thankful.

Anytime I have felt myself about to complain or get down about my situation, I choose to be thankful. First of all, I remind myself that somewhere, someone has it worse than me. Number two, I remind myself of where I came from… that where I am at is far better than where I was. Number three, I know that if I don't protect my peace, I will fail and one way I protect my peace is to be thankful.

Thankfulness in every area of life will always lead to peace in that area. No matter what is going on in your marriage, be thankful for them. Be thankful for the little things they do for you. Be thankful for the material things you do have instead of comparing to what others have. Be thankful for the ministry that God has called you to. Be thankful for the faithful church members that are there every Sunday instead of griping about the ones who show up occasionally - ask me how I know about that one!

When you are thankful for what you have, you will advance in what you have and as you advance, you will find that God will bring increase your way.

DAY 28
FINISH THE WORK

John 4:34 NKJV
Jesus said to them, "My food is to do the will of Him who sent Me, and to finish His work.

Let's be honest…life is hard. It has its challenges, trials, critics, giants, mountains and storms. Even Jesus said in John 6:33, "In this world, you will face troubles, but take courage, for I have conquered the world." So when you take off running down the road to advance, you can cross the starting line knowing that somewhere down the road, there will be some troubles.

Certainly there will be trouble when you do wrong, but just because trouble comes — don't assume it was because you're doing something wrong. In the parable of the sower, Jesus told the disciples that persecution came because of the sake of the Word. When you are putting the Word of God to work, persecution will come. When persecution comes, I take it as a compliment because I know I am being recognized by hell for doing Kingdom business!

Life isn't a sprint; life is a marathon. Anyone can start a marathon but not as many finish it. You have to have something that drives you to finish, especially when you are advancing in the things of God.

Anyone that knows me knows that I am extremely driven. When I lock in to what I need to do, I am locked in; no one is going to change my mind and no one is going to get in my way and stay. If you want to go after greater, if you want to go where no one has gone before, you need a fire burning on the inside of you that cannot be put out.

Jesus gives us a clue as to the driven Man that He was and what fueled that fire. Jesus said, "My food is to do the will of Him who sent me and to finish His work." There are three things I want you to see here. One, Jesus was a man on a mission. He wasn't focused on His plans; He was focused only on God's plans. Two, Jesus knew He was a sent one. When you know you are sent, you know you have a purpose to fulfill. Third, Jesus was driven not just by doing the will of God, but also by finishing the work. This wasn't Jesus' plan and work; this was God's work that Jesus was sent to do and to finish.

Friend, this is what drives me: I am a man on a mission to do what God called me to do and finish it. Until I finish it, I am not done. I will continue advancing until the job is done.

While you are advancing, refuse to quit. Don't look at the troubles; trouble your troubles and keep going! Do the will of God at all costs. Keep your eyes on the finish line and do this one thing: finish the work!

DAY 29
USE YOUR IMAGINATION FOR GOOD

Joshua 1:8 NKJV
This Book of the Law shall not depart from your mouth, but you shall meditate in it day and night, that you may observe to do according to all that is written in it. For then you will make your way prosperous, and then you will have good success.

God wants you to use your imagination for His good! We are great at using our imagination — we just usually use it for the curse. People are great at imagining the worst possible scenarios of bad news. I have literally watched people extremely close to me imagine themselves into sickness because they were constantly allowing their thought life to think about it and be worried about it.

Do you realize that worry is simply you allowing your imagination to run wild with thoughts of doubt and fear? Worrying is simply meditation used for evil instead of meditation or imagination used for good!

After Moses died, Joshua was appointed to be the new leader of the Israelites. In Joshua 1:8, we find some of the instructions God gives to Joshua. One of the things God told Joshua to do was to meditate on the law of God so that He would know what to do and be successful in doing it.

The word *meditate* in Joshua 1:8 is the Hebrew word *Hagah*. Take a wild guess at what it means? Not only does it mean to muse, mutter, meditate, devise, and plot, it also means to imagine.

God's instructions to Joshua was to take His Word and fill His imagination with it and then let His imagination run wild all throughout the day with the Word of God. What would be the result? Joshua would know what needed to be done and he would be successful in doing it.

Notice God didn't instruct Joshua to call a meeting before all of the Israelites and tell them all of God's secrets to him. Today most people would be tempted to quickly post a video on social media to announce the big plans — but that isn't what God told Joshua to do.

One of the most spiritual and beneficial things you can do is to spend time imagining the dreams God has for you. If you are like me, I don't like to sit still — I feel like I need to be doing something. For many years, I felt like I needed to be doing something with my hands in order to accomplish something for the day; however, I found I can accomplish great things with my imagination as well.

If you talk to or read after people that are extremely successful in the business world, you will find two things in common: they spend time reading and they spend time imagining. What would happen in the Church if we would do what God told Joshua to do? The imagination is a subject that you will find throughout the Bible; the problem is people only associate it with evil. However, your imagination is like fire; it can be used for good and it can be used for evil.

God needs you to advance, to increase and to multiply. He needs you to go after greater and so does the world. One year from now, you should be able to look back to this day and see that there has been an increase in the area in which God has called you. The imagination allows you to see the realities of the Kingdom of God and to walk out its realities in this world. Whatever has your imagination will have your faith and whatever has your faith is what will be produced in your life. If you want to go after greater in your life, you will first have to go after greater in your imagination.

DAY 30
LOVE YOUR ENEMIES

> *Matthew 5:43-44 NLT*
> *"You have heard the law that says, 'Love your neighbor' and hate your enemy. But I say, love your enemies! Pray for those who persecute you!*

While you are advancing, you will have your naysayers and critics and then you will have outright enemies. I am talking about people who despise you, hate you, and cringe when they even hear your name.

Unfortunately, I have been on the receiving end of hatred like that — and it's not fun. When I look back at my life, it is interesting that I was well liked in my adult years until I started pushing for more, going for greater, and endeavoring to advance. You start doing some great things for God and all of a sudden, here come the demons!

I remember in the spring of 2019, Covid was hitting America. Right before Easter Sunday, I put up a post on social media about Jesus healing our diseases and bearing Covid-19. You would have thought I said that Santa Claus was Jesus! The post got picked up by a local news station, which got picked up by Newsweek and the next thing I know, my name is in every major newspaper and being talked about by the governor of Arkansas!

People all over the country and in other parts of the world were fighting mad because of the stance I made over a virus - and I am talking about Christians! You wouldn't believe some of the things I had Christians say to me about what I was doing; of course, it got even more vile with the non Christians. I had people calling and sending messages that I needed to die a slow, painful, agonizing death - because not only did I keep my church open, we were inviting people with Covid to come to church to be ministered to!

Friend, how could I preach healing and shut my church down? Why would I be afraid of something Jesus set me free from? How could I be endeavoring to advance in the Kingdom of God, advance in the area of healing and yet, I'm going to close the church because of a virus? Nope! Nope! Nope!

In the midst of hate and the media parking across the street from our church, I chose to love people. Oh, I won't lie—I wanted to hate some of them for what they were doing and saying about me and my family, but I made a decision to love my enemies.

I understood the devil was behind all of this. I was preaching the gospel of Jesus and proving it to people. I was telling people we weren't afraid of the devil's virus. When you tick off the devil, he will go and influence Christian and sinner alike that will allow themselves to be used.

Our fight isn't a physical fight, but a spiritual fight. People are responsible for their actions, but I knew the spirit behind all of this. Mark my words: anytime there is division in a church or an attack against the work of God, it is always demonic. Because of knowing this reality, it made it easier to love people despite what they were doing against me.

Friend, you have to advance; just know that while you are advancing, you will have enemies. When your enemies show their ugly face, just smile at them and say Jesus loves you. Love them, forgive them and move on.

DAY 31
KEEP THE MAIN THING THE MAIN THING

Matthew 6:33 NKJV
But seek first the kingdom of God and His righteousness, and all these things shall be added to you.

In our crazy world, there are many voices. As you are advancing, these voices will try to pull you in lots of directions. There will be various opportunities that will come your way and many opinions from friends and family of what you need to do and where you need to go. But can I give you some advice? Keep the main thing the main thing.

If you want to be successful in doing what God has called you to do, keep the main thing the main thing. There are quite a few things I am good at, but there is one thing that I know I am called to: as a result, it has to be the main thing in my life.

I have watched fellow ministers start off strong in their calling, but then start to flounder because they start getting involved in other things outside of their main thing. There are many areas of society that need born-again, spirit-filled people involved;

however, just because it is a good thing, doesn't mean it is the right thing for you.

It is vitally important that we separate what is the main thing for me and what are good things. For example, it would be a good thing for me to be involved in politics simply because I don't compromise and I would make godly decisions; however, just because it would be a good thing doesn't mean it is the right thing for me. I could get involved in politics, produce movies, start a private school and a host of other good things — but I can only focus on one thing, the main thing that God called me to do.

Jesus tells us to seek first His Kingdom and His righteousness. Well, what is my part in the Kingdom? We have all been called to focus on something — the main thing. If you are struggling in knowing what that is, let me ask you two questions. First, what is your passion in life? Secondly, where have you seen the most success in life? Usually the answer to those two things is what God has graced you to do.

I have watched ministers try to pastor and yet their true calling and prior success is in administration. I have watched pastors try to step out into traveling ministry and as a result, watched their churches begin to go down. Now if God has told you to do it, then go for it because not only will you be satisfied, you will see the fruit that follows! I have also watched businessmen and women try to do ministry when God called them to put making money for the Kingdom first. Just because you can do something well doesn't mean it is the lane God has called you to run in.

In all you do, just make sure and keep the main thing God has called you to do the main thing in which you do. Too many Christians are using a shotgun instead of a rifle. At this point in my life, I am laser focused on the main thing God has called me to. It is the fuel that drives me and I will finish it.

When you are keeping the main thing the main thing, you will be satisfied instead of frustrated. You will find provision with ease instead of struggle. Ultimately, keeping the main thing the main thing will help you to advance into things with a grace that you never thought possible.

DAY 32
CONSCIOUS OF HIS PRESENCE

John 8:29 NKJV
"And He who sent Me is with Me. The Father has not left Me alone, for I always do those things that please Him."

The vast majority of Christians are endeavoring to do a spiritual life conscious of a physical life. This statement is something the Holy Spirit spoke to me while I was doing some writing one day and it was like a slap in the face. It really is one of the number one reasons that we have some of the most intellectual Christians to have ever lived and yet still have limited results. Do you realize how much revelation of the Word of God we have today versus what was prevalent in the last few hundred years?

You can have knowledge of lots of Scripture, but if you do not know the One behind the Scripture, you actually know nothing. We see this with the Pharisees of Jesus' day. They knew the law of God, but they didn't know God.

Years ago, I decided to take everything I had been taught and basically put it on a shelf. I wasn't seeing the results I knew I should be seeing, so I decided to simply go back to the Gospels, especially the book of John and just look at Jesus. I wanted to see what Jesus was saying, doing and thinking. One thing that stood out to me was His reality of God the Father being with Him.

In John 8:29, Jesus says, "He who sent Me is with Me." It's a simple but astounding statement. I want you to notice three things from this:

1. Jesus knew He was a sent One.

2. Jesus knew who sent Him.

3. Jesus knew who was with Him.

God didn't just send Jesus on a mission; God came on the mission with Jesus. Jesus was extremely aware that He was not alone and that the Father was there to help Him. In John 14, Jesus tells the disciples that it is the Father on the inside of Him who was working the miracles. When you listen to Jesus talk about the Father, it literally sounds like He is talking about a real person with Him...no different than if He was talking about Peter, James or John with Him.

Just as God is Jesus' Father, He is our Father. He is a spirit and we are a spirit; as a result, we should be just as aware of Him as we are anything else in this world. If Jesus could be conscious of God with Him, we should be conscious of God with us.

We must work to renew our mind in this area. As we do so, when we face tough times, we will never feel alone. When we stand before impossible situations, we will know the Greater One is with us. When we don't know what to do, we will know the Genius is right there with us.

Friend, don't fall into the religious trap of thinking, praying and singing songs about God coming down to be with you. No, God is with you, and He has never left you. If you aren't aware of

Him, it's not because God has left you, it's because you simply are more conscious of other things than Him.

Spend time throughout your day focusing on the reality that God is with you right now. It is easy to advance and do those things that please Him when you know He is always with you.

DAY 33
STOP CARING

1 Peter 5:6-8 NKJV
Therefore humble yourselves under the mighty hand of God, that He may exalt you in due time, casting all your care upon Him, for He cares for you. Be sober, be vigilant; because your adversary the devil walks about like a roaring lion, seeking whom he may devour.

Caring will kill you. It's a bold statement, but friend, I've watched it play out in people's lives. People think that caring is a mature thing, but it's actually a demonic thing and if not dealt with, it will takeover your life. I've watched it happened firsthand to people I loved. Care is purely of the devil and it is designed to do one thing: devour you.

In 1 Peter 5, we find a powerful truth about the subject of cares. First of all, caring is a form of pride. When you take on cares, you take on the role of God in your life. You basically kick God off the throne in your life and try to take His place of being your provider and protector. Care is simply worry with makeup; it is fear dressed up to look harmless - but it will kill you.

Second, notice that the apostle Peter says, "Casting all of your care upon Him for He cares for you." This may sound strange that we are told not to care, but God is allowed to care. Let me show you something in the Greek. The two "cares" used here are different words. When he says, "Cast all of your cares," in the Greek, it is really referring to anxieties that are meant to distract you. When he says, "God cares for you," this care is referring to an object of affection or interest. What he is telling us is that we need to get rid of our fears, anxieties and worries because God is looking out for us to provide for us.

Third, notice that immediately after telling you to humble yourself by giving your cares and worries to God, he informs you that satan is going about looking for people to devour. Friend, according to this passage of Scripture in 1 Peter, who is it that satan can devour? Satan can devour the person who is full of cares. Notice, there is no exception here to whether the person is a minister, how long they have been saved, what they have accomplished for God, etc, - none of these things matter! The only qualifier to whether satan can devour the Christian is ONE THING: CARES.

Satan has no authority in the life of the Christian. He literally can do nothing to you until you open the door to cares. Certainly we are to care for our children, care for our business or ministry, care about our home and finances; but that caring is not to be anxieties that distract us from God our Provider - the caring is simply to be that these are people/ things of interest in our lives.

There are a lot of Christians that will criticize a drunkard thats full of alcohol, but won't hold the same standard to the person drunk on their cares. We are to be sober. You can be just as drunk on booze as you can on cares; both of them will keep you out of your right mind and both will potentially kill you.

You will never advance in life while burdened with cares - because I am telling you right now, those cares will bury you and you'll never get to finish what God called you to do. Be sober, vigilant and humble. Refuse to care so that God can care for you.

DAY 34
BUILT DIFFERENT

2 Timothy 2:3 NKJV
You therefore must endure hardship as a good soldier of Jesus Christ.

I have always loved movies about the underdog; movies about the person who comes from nothing, faces obstacles that would make most people falter, and then comes out on top. One characteristic about the people in these stories is that you find they are just resilient; nothing can stop them. There are some people that are just built differently in their soul.

The Bible says in 2 Timothy 2:3 that we are to endure hardships like a good soldier of Christ. You'll find that good soldiers are able to take the hard times that come, brush them off and keep going because there is a mission to fulfill. One of my favorite movies is *Hacksaw Ridge* directed by Mel Gibson. It is an extraordinary true story of Desmond Doss, who saved seventy-five men in Okinawa during the bloodiest battle of WWII without firing a single shot. When you watch the movie, you see that he wasn't a big, burly soldier; he was small, but his heart was huge. What he accomplished on that ridge in Okinawa is absolutely amazing, but it didn't come because of his strength or skills; it came because he was just "built different."

This is a phrase that Jake and I have adopted. I remember one day Jake and I were talking about some of the hard things we have been through and how we have kept going. Jake said, "Dad, we're just built different." I looked at him and said, "Buddy, you are right."

If you want to advance, you have to be built different. We are all going to experience hardships and unfortunately, some of us will even experience loss, but despite what comes our way, we are to give our cares to the Lord and keep marching forward. Being built different doesn't mean that we do not feel emotional hurts and pains; it simply means that I will not allow the hurts and cares of this world to determine my personality, my outlook on life and the day I will experience.

There is an attitude of a soldier we must have: we fight to the finish, no matter the cost. Friend, you may have gone through hard times, but you can do it. Be built different in your soul. Be a good soldier and stay focused on the mission Jesus has sent you to accomplish. No matter what comes our way, we choose to continue to advance.

DAY 35

THE HEART OF A GIVER

Proverbs 11:24-25 NLT
Give freely and become more wealthy; be stingy and lose everything. The generous will prosper; those who refresh others will themselves be refreshed.

It doesn't matter who you are, we all need money. As you advance, you are going to need more money. I'll never forget several years ago, I was in a meeting with Jesse Duplantis. While he was preaching, he came up to me and had me stand up. He said, "Chad, you are not believing big enough. What the Lord is calling you to is going to cost you more money than you think."

It didn't make much sense to me because of the phase of ministry I was in; little did I know that a few months later, the Lord would have me turn over my church and step into the phase of ministry that I am in today. This phase of ministry is costing me more money now than when I was pastoring and yet, every year that we advance further, it has cost more money.

The good thing is that money is not a problem with God. He actually has a spiritual law in place to enable us to access everything we will ever need. It is the law of sowing and reaping.

In Proverbs, we find wisdom from the wisest man and the richest man to have ever lived before Jesus; this man's name was Solomon. In Proverbs 11, Solomon says, "Give freely and you will become more wealthy." It goes totally contrary to the world's way of increase, but this is about the Kingdom way. Now I am not talking about just frivolously giving all of your money away because you want more. You can do the right thing with the wrong motivation and it can end up being wrong.

When it comes to teaching on giving, I always told our church this: "We give with a purpose and with a promise." The purpose of our giving is to honor God, show our thanksgiving and be a blessing to other people. The promise on our giving is that we will prosper in what we have given. The purpose is our motivating factor; the promise is simply a byproduct of the purpose.

I absolutely love to give. It truly is more of a blessing to give than it is to receive. Each year I have stretched myself to give more and more. Over the years, I have watched that every single time I have given my largest financial seed at the direction of the Lord, I have watched it come back in abundance. I'm not giving to get; I am giving to give. However, this is also how you increase. Friend, I'm telling you just like Jesse told me, "You are not believing big enough. You are going to need more money than you think!"

The plans God has for you - it is going to take money and the further you go, the more money you will need. But I want you to do this - focus on the call of God and focus on being a blessing to people. No one has ever out given God. If you want to advance the Kingdom of God, you will have to advance your finances too.

Be a giver and watch how money advances to you as you advance the Kingdom!

DAY 36
UNTOUCHABLE

Psalm 91:9-10 NKJV
Because you have made the Lord, who is my refuge, Even the Most High, your dwelling place, No evil shall befall you, Nor shall any plague come near your dwelling.

Let's face the fact: you can't advance if you are sick. What happens to sick people? They stop working and start sleeping. You become focused on your body and not on the mission.

Jesus tells us in John 17 that in the same way God sent Jesus to the earth on a mission, Jesus has sent you to the earth on a mission. Now, tell me this: where was Jesus sick? Don't get religious and tell me Jesus didn't get sick because He was God. Jesus was God, but He was doing life in every way as a man (Philippians 2:5-8). Jesus was doing life as a man anointed by God, united with God, filled with God and with a covenant with God.

We can see that part of this covenant included not just healing, but the absence of sickness. Did you see what I said there? The Church world that actually believes in healing has preached that

God will heal you, but our covenant with God actually goes further than that! Our covenant with God says that we won't get sick! Look at Psalm 91. Read through it and tell me where it says God will heal you. No, it says, "No plague will come near your dwelling."

Friend, I want you to know this! This world is filled with sickness and incurable diseases. There is evil in the world and man made diseases that are coming down the pipeline that will have no medications or vaccines available. Satan will do everything he can to try and stop you from advancing - even going to the point of starting a pandemic of disease.

Do you know what we are going to do in the midst of the next health pandemic? While one thousand falls at one side and ten thousand at another side, we keep advancing free of disease. I never got COVID because I can't get sick. I don't say that arrogantly; I say that because the Bible tells me this! As we continue to advance, I'm telling you this boldly and blatantly: diseases and the fear of diseases will continue to rise - BUT WHERE SIN ABOUNDS, GRACE ABOUNDS EVEN MORE.

I want you to take on this attitude and perspective starting today - and be bold about it: "It is impossible for me to be sick."

Through salvation, Jesus made you dead to sin and dead to sickness. It is good news! You can live the rest of your life free of disease so you can advance the Kingdom of God and fulfill all He has called you to do!

DAY 37
CONFORMED

Romans 12:2 NKJV
And do not be conformed to this world, but be transformed by the renewing of your mind, that you may prove what is that good and acceptable and perfect will of God.

You can't advance when you think like everyone else. Advanced living requires advanced thinking. Remember, you have to be built different; yet, to be built different means you have to think differently.

The apostle Paul gave a strong command when he told the Romans, "Do not be conformed to this world." This command is not just about your behaviors and values. Far too often people use this scripture to talk only about sin. Certainly, we need to lay aside the sin and weights that will hold us back, but sin isn't the only thing that will hold you back - cursed thinking will hold you back even more!

People who do not see things from Heaven's perspective have cursed thinking. These people still see themselves as alive unto the curse and dependent on the world's systems. The will of God is Heaven on earth. Notice we are to change the way we think so we can prove the will of God. This isn't about God proving anything; this is about you proving the will of God; you manifesting the perfect will of God in every area of your life.

If there is an area of your life that doesn't look like Heaven, it is because your mind is not renewed to see like Heaven in that area. This is why we are told in Colossians 3:1-3 to set our mind on the realities of Heaven, where Christ is, because we have died to the things of this world. Friend, you have to see yourself as a dead person to the curse. The curse can't touch you because you are dead to it! The limitations of the world's systems can't limit you because you are dead to it!

God needs you to think differently so people can experience differently. Remember, as a man thinks in his heart, so he is (Proverbs 23:7). Start thinking like Heaven so you can start experiencing some Heaven!

DAY 38
SURROUND YOURSELF WITH BIG THINKERS

Proverbs 27:17 NLT
As iron sharpens iron, so a friend sharpens a friend.

Remember how we said that advanced living requires advanced thinking? Well, we were never called to do life alone and in order for you to advance in your thinking, you need people around you to help you. When I made the decision to start advancing and truly push past the status quo, I desperately began to search out those who were getting more results than me. I didn't care what group they were in, what denomination they were a part of, or where they went to Bible school… if they were getting better results than me, then I wanted to know what were they thinking and what were they doing.

Those people that were willing to talk to me, I would take full advantage of it and ask questions. There were times I drove for hours just to spend a few minutes with someone.

If I was unable to talk to them personally, I would get any of their books or videos that were available simply to learn from them.

I remember when I first started out in ministry, almost all of the people I was around were all small thinkers. I began to look at what they were involved in and realized it was all small; their plans were small, but their complaints were big!

I remember one time I was invited to a meeting of pastors across the city. One of the pastors invited me to come because he knew I had just graduated bible school and was about to start a church; he thought it would be good for me to sit and learn. Well, I went one time and in the first 15 minutes of this pastor's meeting, I learned something quick: I need to get out of here. It was just complaining and excuses from all of them!

I needed someone made of iron; not cloth. I needed someone of strength to help sharpen me. Eventually, I found a few people that thought bigger than me and were pushing to go further. Do you know what happened? I started growing and as a result, my results started growing.

In many ways, you are a product of your environment; as the saying goes, "You are who you hang with." I have purposely surrounded myself with big thinkers. Why? I want to advance! To advance big, you need to think big! You need big thinking and you need to be around big thinkers. You need to be extremely cautious who you listen to for advice. Don't be listening to people who think small; they will stop your advancement. Find those who have advanced beyond you or at least are thinking beyond your scope of thinking. You may not have personal access to them, but in the age we live in, you can learn from people through their books and videos.

Be purposeful in who your mentors are. Be purposeful in who you read after and listen to. Be purposeful in who you spend your time with. Show me who you hang with and I will show you where you are headed.

DAY 39
BE STILL

Psalm 46:10 NLT
Be still, and know that I am God!

I have always been someone who had a hard time just being still; not from the standpoint of being restless, but from the standpoint of needing to accomplish something. Even when I'm sitting down, so many times, my mind is still running at full speed, thinking about what needs to be done, what could be done, or how we could do something better. April will tell you that I am always visioneering.

Over the years, while I have continued to advance, one thing that has helped me greatly has been learning how to be still and enjoy the quiet moments. So many of us have gotten to a place where we need to have music playing all the time, a television on or some type of noise in the background. However, we must realize that where there is always noise, rarely is there peace.

In Psalm 46:10, God said, "Be still and know that I am God!" Notice, He didn't say, "Find a noisy place and know that I am

God." He didn't say, "Get busy and know that I am God." He said, "Be still."

I have found that the quiet times of life have been the easiest time to not only hear from God but be aware of Him. God understands that we have lives to live, families to take care of, and jobs to do. This issue of being still isn't necessarily always about being by yourself, hidden away in a closet; much of being still is learning to be still in your mind.

We can get to a place where even during our busy times, we can maintain a sense of peace and stillness in our thoughts and emotions. Maintaining stillness in our thoughts and emotions does not come overnight; this comes from staying in this place day in and day out.

Those that are very close to me will tell you that I am always harping on this one thing: protect your peace. In my office and in my home, you will almost always find soft, peaceful music playing. Now I certainly love some good upbeat stuff, but I am always endeavoring to keep my my mind still and at rest. I refuse to get into arguments or get offended because I want to keep my mind still and at rest. There is nothing in this world important enough to lose my stillness. Be still and know God; this is what we need.

As I have gotten older, I have learned to enjoy quiet times. On long drives by myself, I am usually driving in quiet; no music on, simply praying in tongues. I will go on walks by myself or just go sit on the beach or go to the woods and sit and listen. There is just something about getting alone for a time for the simple reason to be still.

As you are advancing, things are going to get busier. I am busier now than I have ever been before, but I am also more conscious of my time and the busyness. I have learned to delegate more and set aside more time to be still. I have become very intentional about my soul control, refusing to care, refusing to worry and maintaining my peace.

If I want to fulfill all God has called me to do, I can't do it without knowing Him and being conscious of Him. It is from that consciousness of Him that faith flows and advancement goes.

DAY 40
FORGET THE PAST

Philippians 3:13-14 NKJV
No, dear brothers and sisters, I have not achieved it, but I focus on this one thing: Forgetting the past and looking forward to what lies ahead, I press on to reach the end of the race and receive the heavenly prize for which God, through Christ Jesus, is calling us.

Every day that we advance, we will take new ground. Every day that we advance, we will see more miracles. Every day that we advance, we will accomplish more and experience more. With these advancements, there will be trials and there will be victories; however, in order for us to continue to advance, we must take the wins and the losses and put them in the past.

No sports team wins a second championship while they are celebrating their first championship. When you have a victory, you celebrate it, lay it aside and then you push forward. It is the same in business, ministry and in life.

The Apostle Paul accomplished many great things, yet despite everything he had accomplished, he made this statement: "Forget the past and look forward to what lies ahead."

I don't care what you have accomplished, how many trophies you have in your trophy case, how many followers you have on social media, or how many best selling books you have published — there is no prize greater than what is at the end of our advancement. When we have advanced what God has called us to do, finished the work as a good soldier and stand before Jesus, we will hear those words, "Well done, my good and faithful servant."

I don't want to stand before Jesus and be told my believing was too small. I don't want to find out I could have done more. I want to know that I stretched myself, advanced past what the world and church said was possible and took Him at His Word.

Friend, as you advance, there will be applause and there will be jeers; there will be trials and there will be triumphs. As you advance, it will bring you before people and it will bring some success. However, I am not interested in being famous; I am interested in being faithful.

We celebrate the successes, learn from the failures and we keep going with our eyes on the prize. The prize is not fame and fortune; the prize is being called faithful.

Let this drive your advancement. Know that Jesus is counting on you, the Church is counting on you and the world is counting on you. There is coming a day very soon when all that you thought important in this world will become unimportant. All the material things you strived for will be burned up. There will be one thing that will be priceless; knowing you did what Jesus called you to do.

Be faithful my friend. Find what God has called you to do and advance in it like no man or woman in Christ has ever done before. Together, let's go after greater.

Always advancing. Always increasing. Always multiplying.

It is time to advance.

ABOUT THE AUTHOR

Chad Gonzales is a passionate visionary with a mission to elevate the Church to the standard set by Jesus Himself. His heart's desire is for believers to awaken to their true identity in Christ and manifest Heaven on Earth as children of God. With a strong emphasis on identity in Christ and the ministry of healing, Chad fearlessly declares the Word of God, resulting in frequent miraculous healings in his ministry, including restored sight, hearing, and even the dissolution of tumors.

As the founder of The Healing Academy, Chad has devoted his life to helping individuals unlock their divine potential and experience the supernatural. His extensive educational background includes a Master of Education in Counseling from Lamar University and a Doctorate of Ministry from the School of Bible Theology Seminary and University, equipping him with a profound understanding of the human mind and spirit.

With over two decades of pastoral and church-planting experience, Chad intimately understands the needs and struggles of believers, providing practical guidance and support. He is also a prolific author, known for empowering believers with books like "The Supernatural Prayer of Jesus: Secrets from the Son of God That Unleash The Miracle Realm."

Based in vibrant Tampa, Florida, Chad serves as the driving force behind Chad Gonzales Ministries, where he continues to write captivating books and contributes to the development of

Union University, an innovative online Bible school designed to offer comprehensive spiritual education worldwide.

Through his teachings, programs, and media platforms such as The Way Of Life television program and The Supernatural Life Podcast, Chad has left an indelible mark on the lives of thousands both nationally and internationally. He is a living testament to the miraculous power of faith and the boundless possibilities that await those who dare to believe.

To learn more about Chad Gonzales and his ministry, visit www.chadgonzales.com. Join him on a journey to embrace the supernatural and walk in the footsteps of Jesus.

ALSO BY CHAD GONZALES

Advance

Aliens

An Alternate Reality

Believing God For A House

Eight Percent

Fearless

God's Will Is You Healed

Making Right Decisions

Naturally Supernatural

Possessors of Life

The Supernatural Prayer of Jesus

Think Like Jesus

Walking In The Miraculous

THE SUPERNATURAL LIFE PODCAST

Check out *The Supernatural Life Podcast* with Chad Gonzales! New episodes are available each month designed to help you connect with God on a deeper level and live the supernatural life God desires for you to have.

THE HEALING ACADEMY

The Healing Academy is an outreach of Chad Gonzales Ministries to help the everyday believer learn to walk according to the standard of Jesus in the ministry of healing.

Jesus said in John 14:12 that whoever believes in Him would do the same works and even greater works. Through The Healing Academy, it is our goal to raise the standard of the healing ministry in the Church and manifest the ministry of Jesus in the marketplace.

The Healing Academy is available online as well as in person training. For more information, please visit thehealingacademy.com.

MORE FROM CGM

Looking to attend a Live event with Chad? Visit chadgonzales.com/schedule or scan the QR code to find an event near you.

Printed in Poland
by Amazon Fulfillment
Poland Sp. z o.o., Wrocław